The Value of TENACITY

The Story of Maurice Richard

VALUE COMMUNICATIONS, INC.
PUBLISHERS
LA JOLLA, CALIFORNIA

The Value of TENACITY

ILLUSTRATED BY Pileggi

The Story of
Maurice Richard
BY ANN DONEGAN JOHNSON

First Edition
Manufactured in the United States of America.
For information write to: ValueTales,
9601 Arrow Drive, San Diego, CA 92123

All dialogue in the text is fictitious.

Library of Congress Cataloging in Publication Data

Johnson, Anne Donegan.
    The value of tenacity.

    (ValueTales series)
    SUMMARY: A biography of Maurice Richard, whose
tenacity in the face of many injuries helped him become
one of Canada's finest hockey players.
    1. Richard, Maurice, 1921–   —Juvenile literature.
2. Hockey players—Canada—Biography—Juvenile literature.
(1. Richard, Maurice, 1921– . 2. Hockey players.
3. Persistence) I. Title. II. Series.
GV848.5.R5J66   1983   796.96′2′0924 [B] [92]   84-8972

ISBN 0-7172-8134-4

A 84

This is the story of Maurice Richard, who,
thanks to his tenacity and his enthusiasm,
became one of the best hockey players of our
time. The story that follows is based on
events in his life. His biography can be found
on page 63.

Once upon a time...

not so very long ago, an eight-year-old boy leaned on a window sill and looked out at the wintry Montreal morning. His name was Maurice Richard.

"I'm glad we live in this house," he said to himself, smiling. It wasn't a very beautiful house, and it wasn't very big. But it was warm and cozy, and Maurice liked it.

Even better than the house itself, Maurice liked the backyard, with its small skating rink.

Maurice remembered the cold Saturday a month before when his father had said, "If you and your friends will help, we can make a skating rink in the backyard today."

What hard work it had been for Maurice and his friends! First, side boards had to be cut and nailed into place. But that part was easy compared to what came next: they began the long, slow job of flooding the rink. They had to wait for one layer of ice to freeze, then add another and another.

As the hours passed, Maurice's friends gave up. One by one, they went home. Maurice and his father were left to finish the job.

Finally, Maurice was ready to give up too. His mittens were crusted with ice and his fingers were numb with cold. "Dad," he said, "I want to go in. I'm frozen. We're never going to finish flooding the rink today."

"Maurice," answered his father, "no one ever gets ahead who quits when the going gets tough." Nodding towards the window where the younger Richard children were watching them, he added, "You're the oldest in the family. You have to set a good example to your brothers and sisters. Show that you can get a job done if you stick to it."

So Maurice stayed until the rink was finished. By then it was dark, and the younger children had eaten and gone to bed. In the cozy warmth of the kitchen, Maurice ate the good, thick soup his mother had kept hot for him. He forgot the miserable hours he had just spent. "That was great soup, Mom," said Maurice, patting his stomach. "Is it okay if I try the rink now?"

"Maurice!" his mother protested. "You came in absolutely frozen only half an hour ago. You can't possibly want to go out in the cold again!"

But Maurice did want to go out, and his mother felt he had earned a reward for his hard work. "All right," she smiled, "but it's bedtime, so no more than fifteen minutes!"

Maurice would never forget that night. How wonderful it felt to glide over the new ice under a crisp, starry, winter sky! "Dad was right," he thought. "I am sure glad I stayed on to finish the rink. It was worth being cold."

"But that was a month ago," thought Maurice suddenly as he sat at the window. "Why waste time dreaming about that night when I could be out skating now?"

It was very early in the morning, only a little past six. The rest of the family was still asleep. Quickly Maurice struggled into warm pants and layer after layer of sweaters. In Montreal, the winters can be very cold.

He crept silently downstairs. Quickly, he laced on his skates. He stuffed a hockey puck into his pocket and looked over at his brand new hockey stick leaning against the door.

"Come on, Slapper," he said, "let's go play hockey."

Maurice hadn't told anyone that he had given his stick a name. He was afraid they would think he was silly. "But Slapper suits you perfectly," he said to the stick as he picked it up. "That's the sound you make when you hit the puck . . . SLAP!"

Having a name for his stick made Maurice feel that he was skating with a friend.

Carefully, Maurice opened the door and went outside. He skated twice around the small rink to warm up. Soon he was aiming the puck at the wooden crate that he used as a goal net.

Maurice shot. "He scores!" he cried, pretending that he was playing at the Forum for his favorite team, the Montreal Canadiens. To Maurice, the Canadiens were the best hockey team in Canada, the best in the world. Like most of the children in his neighborhood, he could imagine nothing more glorious than to someday play for the Canadiens.

The Richards didn't have enough money to go to the Forum to watch the Canadiens play, but every Saturday night the whole family gathered around the radio and listened to "Hockey Night in Canada." Although Maurice had never seen his heroes, he felt that he had played every game with them.

Wham! Maurice tripped on some rough ice and skidded along the rink. "Darn! That's what I get for daydreaming. Oh, what's the use anyway? I'll never be good enough to play hockey with the Canadiens."

Suddenly, Maurice thought he heard a little voice. "You're wrong, Maurice," it said. "You can play with the Canadiens when you grow up if you really want to and if you work hard enough at it."

"What?" said Maurice, startled.

"I said that you can do it," the voice went on. "All you need is tenacity."

Maurice raised his head to find out who was talking. Who do you think it was?

That's right. It was Slapper, lying on the ice beside him. Maurice couldn't believe his eyes or ears. His brand new hockey stick seemed to be talking to him.

"Tenacity means sticking with it, refusing to give up no matter what," Slapper explained, giving Maurice a little time to recover from his surprise.

Of course, Maurice knew that hockey sticks don't really talk. He knew it was really his own thoughts he was listening to. It didn't matter, he liked what he heard.

"Do you really think I can play with the Canadiens one day?"

"Sure you can" replied Slapper. "Not if you lie around chatting on the ice, though. Come on. Get up and start practicing. That's all it takes . . . practice, practice, practice."

"Slapper's right about that," thought Maurice. "After all, even the top players have to practice. I've heard them say so on the radio."

From that day on, Maurice practiced skating and shooting the puck every chance he could get. And his friend Slapper was always with him.

On cold school days, Maurice would lace on his skates after breakfast, grab Slapper and meet his friends at the end of the street. They'd skate to school over the ice-covered roads, shooting the puck back and forth as they went.

At noon Maurice would skate home and beg his mother to let him eat lunch with his skates on. That way he didn't have to waste time taking them off and putting them on again. After lunch he could skate for a few minutes on the backyard rink before he had to go back to school. Sometimes, when it was his turn to help with the dishes, his mother would take pity on him. "Go ahead, son," she'd say. "You can help another time."

After school the Richards' rink was filled with the neighborhood boys playing hockey.

For Maurice, the best times were when his father came with him to the frozen river behind the house after dinner.

"Hey Dad, watch this," Maurice would cry.

Then he would skate as hard and fast as he could to show his father how much he was improving. Mr. Richard was very proud of his son. "He skates like a rocket," he would say to anyone who would listen, as Maurice whooshed by with Slapper.

"Like a rocket," whispered Slapper to Maurice. "Do you hear that, Maurice?"

Maurice didn't say anything. He just smiled to himself because sometimes, especially on the river at night, he felt like a rocket streaking through the starry skies.

Maurice always felt sad when spring arrived. He hated to watch the ice on the river break up. Standing on the river bank with Slapper beside him, Maurice sighed. "I'll never be good enough to play with the Canadiens if I have to give up practicing now."

"Yes you will," replied Slapper. "But you'll have to take up other sports to keep fit. What about baseball or swimming or boxing? You can do them all summer long. And when next winter comes, you'll be in top shape."

So that's what Maurice did. By the end of the summer he was such a good baseball player that his friends said to him, "Maurice, why don't you give up hockey and just play baseball?"

But Maurice didn't want to give up hockey. He loved streaking across the ice with Slapper. Besides, he had his secret dream. "Someday I'm going to play with the Canadiens," he would say to himself when he was tired and cold after a hard practice.

"That's the spirit, Maurice," Slapper would say, cheering him on. "All it takes is tenacity."

Maurice eventually grew too big to use Slapper, but he never outgrew him as a friend. It was always through Slapper that he heard the voice of his own basic toughness and determination.

Over the next few years Maurice skated and played hockey whenever he could. Soon he was playing on a neighborhood team, learning to dodge the other players and scoop up the puck when it was passed by a teammate.

When he was about fourteen, Maurice began to take an interest in individual Canadien players. His favorite was Toe Blake, who was fast becoming the team's best scorer. "If I could be like Toe Blake!" thought Maurice. "If I could be good enough, someday, to play *with* him!" And to realize that dream, Maurice practiced harder than ever.

Maurice was now studying to be a machinist at Montreal Technical High School. He was a good student and a hard worker, but his heart wasn't really in his studies. He kept thinking about the skating rink, where he spent every spare minute.

In order to play as much hockey as possible, Maurice signed up with several teams at once. This was not really allowed, but at that time officials didn't apply the rules very strictly.

Of course, the other players knew Maurice was doing this, but they never complained. In fact they admired the way Maurice would play hard in a game for one team, then hurry to another rink for a game

with yet another team. Besides, Maurice was one of the best players around; everybody wanted to play with him.

Sometimes, though, his friends teased Maurice about his single-minded devotion to hockey.

"Aw, come on, Maurice," they would say when, after a hard practice session, Maurice would want to keep on playing. "There are other things in life besides hockey, you know."

"Don't tell him that," others would cry in mock alarm. "If he ever finds out, he may stop scoring so many goals!"

One of the players who teased Maurice was Georges Norchet. But Georges, however much he might tease, was one of Maurice's greatest admirers. Watching Maurice score yet another goal, Georges would shake his head in wonder. "He still skates and scores as if it were no problem when the rest of us are too tired to play any more."

Georges raved about Maurice at home too. "He's amazing," Georges told his sister Lucille one day. "Sometimes he plays two games a night! And that's after a full day of school. And he's good too—one of the best. If our team ends up with twelve goals, you can bet Maurice scored ten of them."

Lucille started going to the games to watch Georges and this Maurice Richard. Soon she admired Maurice as much as his teammates did.

One of Maurice's coaches, Paul Stuart, was impressed too. He thought it was time Maurice played on a better team. "The only way you're going to improve," he told Maurice, "is to play with—and against—players who are better than you are.

Coach Stuart called an old friend of his, Arthur Therrien, from the Verdun Maple Leafs, one of Montreal's best junior teams. The friend agreed to let Maurice try out.

Maurice was thrilled. He practiced harder than ever. He made the team, and within two years he was one of its top goal scorers. Georges Norchet and his sister Lucille went to almost every game to cheer Maurice on.

One night Maurice got his big chance. The coach of the Canadiens' Senior team was watching the game from the stands. When he saw how fast Maurice skated and how well he handled the puck, he invited the young player to try out for his team.

Maurice was so excited that he could hardly wait to tell Slapper. Finally the dressing room was empty and he was alone with his old friend.

"Do you realize what it means, Slapper?" he asked after breaking the news. "It's still amateur hockey, but in a couple of years I'll have a chance to try out for Toe Blake's team—the Canadiens!"

Suddenly Maurice's face clouded over. "The Seniors have 125 other players trying out too, though. Most of them are probably better than I am."

"You mustn't think that way, Maurice," Slapper scolded. "You can do it if you have tenacity. When you think of giving up, just grit your teeth and keep playing. That's that way to make the team."

At the Seniors' training camp, Maurice remembered Slapper's words. Often he would feel too tired to skate another inch, but he would say to himself, "Tenacity, Maurice. You have to have tenacity."

And Maurice persevered and practiced harder and longer—and he made the team!

Slapper was overjoyed for him. "That's my boy!" he said. "Have patience, Maurice. Before long you'll be skating beside Toe Blake."

But then, in his first game with the Canadien Seniors, all Maurice's hopes were dashed.

The game started out well for Maurice—he scored two goals in the first two periods. He was working on a third when another player tripped him. Maurice skidded across the ice and crashed into the boards in a corner of the rink. His ankle was broken.

Back in the dressing room, when the doctor had finished setting the broken bone, Maurice had to fight back tears. His first game and he'd broken his ankle! Now he wouldn't be able to play for the rest of the season. Who knows, perhaps he would never be able to play again.

"Maybe I should give up hockey right now and be a machinist," he said quietly.

"No way, Maurice," said Slapper. "You've worked too hard to give it all up as soon as the going gets tough. Have more tenacity, my friend."

Maurice wasn't convinced, but the weeks passed and his ankle healed and he realized Slapper was right. He had to give it another try.

He was able to play in the last few games of the season, and it felt wonderful to be back on the ice. What's more, Lucille Norchet was up in the stands, and that made Maurice feel even better.

In his second year with the Seniors, Maurice quickly proved himself to be a fine young hockey player with a lot of determination.

Then . . . another accident!

It was the twenty-first game of the season. Maurice lost his balance for a moment and reached out to grab the net to stop his fall. His wrist banged into one of the posts and *snap*! The bone broke.

It seemed like the end of Maurice's dream. People were beginning to say he was accident-prone, and no wonder. Two bad injuries in two seasons! He had spent more time off the ice than on.

"Toe Blake's Canadiens will never invite me to skate with them now," he thought. "They'll think I'm too much of a risk." Maurice even thought seriously about giving up his hockey career.

Both Slapper and Lucille Norchet tried to talk him out of the idea. Finally Lucille said, "At least promise me that you will think about it over the summer."

Maurice promised, but nothing seemed to cheer him up.

Then something happened that changed everything. A letter arrived asking Maurice to come to the Canadiens' training camp in the fall. If they liked his style, Maurice would have a good chance of becoming a Canadien.

A chance to try out for the Montreal Canadiens!
A chance to play on Toe Blake's team!

Maurice didn't know it, but the first morning of training camp Coach Irvin was going to put him to the test. Irvin knew about Maurice's injuries. He wanted to be sure Maurice was strong enough to play professional hockey with the Canadiens.

Irvin spoke to one of the team's toughest players, Murph "Hard Rock" Chamberlain. "Go after him hard, Murph. Really make his head spin. I want to see if he can take it."

"Sure thing, Coach," said Murph. And as Maurice skated down the ice with the puck, Murph went after him, smashing him into the boards with all his strength.

Gasping for breath as he lay on the ice, Maurice remembered another fall he had taken years ago on the Richards' backyard rink. He thought for a minute that he could hear Slapper speaking: "Tenacity, Maurice, means sticking with it no matter what."

Maurice hauled himself up onto his feet and skated back into the game. At the edge of the rink, Coach Irvin smiled to himself.

While he was at the Canadiens' training camp, Maurice really had to work hard. The Second World War was raging at the time, and young men who weren't in the armed forces were needed in factories. Maurice had tried to join the army but had been turned down because of damage caused by his broken ankle. He was working long hours in a factory during the day and then playing hockey at night, sometimes until after midnight.

On the last day of training camp, the players waited outside Coach Irvin's office to find out who had been chosen to play with the Canadiens.

The coach finally appeared, holding the list of those who had made the team. He tacked it to the bulletin board, and the players crowded round to see.

There, at the top of the list, was the name "Maurice Richard."

"Welcome to the Montreal Canadiens, Maurice," said Coach Irvin as Maurice turned away from the bulletin board, a huge smile lighting up his face.

Maurice was so happy he could barely stammer out, "Thank you, Mr. Irvin."

Back in the locker room, Slapper was ecstatic. "You've done it, Maurice! You've done it! Thanks to hard work and sticking with it, you've earned a chance to play with Toe Blake."

Maurice then hurried home to tell the news to his bride. That's right, just two weeks earlier Maurice had got married. Can you guess who he married? Of course. Who else but his most faithful fan, Lucille Norchet? Lucille was as thrilled at the wonderful news as Maurice himself.

Finally the season started. As Maurice skated out onto the ice to warm up before the first game, his hero, Toe Blake, glided past. Maurice's dream had come true: he, Maurice Richard, was skating at the Montreal Forum with Toe Blake.

Maurice loved the way the crowd cheered and clapped when he scored a goal. His greatest thrill of all, though, was when Toe Blake slapped him on the back and said, "Congratulations, kid."

By the sixteenth game of the season, Maurice had scored five goals for the Canadiens. He was getting better with every game. And then something very sad happened.

Maurice was skating fast and trying for another goal. Suddenly, a player from the other team crashed into him. He heard a familiar snap. His ankle had broken again.

Maurice was carried off the ice. He was terribly unhappy because he knew that, for him, the season was over. And what about next season? "Oh, Slapper," he said, when they were alone, "do you think the Canadiens will want to keep a player who's always getting hurt?"

The next day, after he read the newspapers, Maurice felt even worse. They were full of stories about his injury. Many sports writers said that they thought Maurice was too fragile to play professional hockey.

This time Slapper and Lucille had an even harder time cheering him up. Maurice knew that he was able to recover from an injury and play hockey better than ever. But would the team give him another chance?

A few days later Coach Irvin called him into his office. Maurice hobbled in on his crutches, expecting to hear that he was fired.

Imagine his joy when Coach Irvin asked him to attend training camp again the next fall. He was still on the team!

"I thought you might not want me after this injury," Maurice said to the coach.

"You should give us more credit, Maurice. We don't give up any more easily than you do."

That next season, Maurice was so happy to be back with the team that he played as hard as he could, never giving up even when he was exhausted.

As he started scoring more goals, the sports writers began to pay more attention to him. They wrote long stories about him in their newspapers.

But Maurice wasn't scoring goals to become famous. He was doing it to help his team and to repay Coach Irvin, who had given him a second chance.

The better Maurice played, the harder the players on other teams worked to stop him from scoring goals. Two or three players would shadow his every move. Instead of being discouraged by the difficulties they created, Maurice simply applied himself harder than ever and learned new ways of getting around them.

One day at practice, one of his teammates gave Maurice the nickname that stuck with him the rest of his life. Toe Blake, Maurice and Elmer Lach were trying to get past three of their own teammates to score a goal. As Maurice whizzed towards them, one of them yelled: "Here comes the Rocket!"

After the practice was over Slapper said to Maurice: "Rocket Richard. That's a good name for you, Maurice. Remember when your father said you skated like a rocket?"

Soon all the newspapers were full of stories about the Rocket.

One story told of a spectacular goal he scored in his third year with the Canadiens in a game against the Detroit Red Wings.

It all started when Maurice broke away from the other players and tore down the ice with the puck. A Detroit player took off after him, but the Rocket was too fast. Since he couldn't get in front of Maurice to stop him, the other player leapt on Maurice's back.

Maurice almost collapsed under the weight of the Detroit player. "I'm so close to the goal, I can't give up now," he said to himself. So Maurice piggybacked the other player towards the goal. He shot the puck into the net with a resounding slap, and the crowd roared their approval. Nothing could stop the Rocket!

The same year as the famous piggyback goal, Maurice scored more goals in the play-offs than any hockey player ever had before. With his help, the Canadiens won the Stanley cup, the trophy given every year to the best team in the league.

The next year, the Canadiens won the Cup again, and Maurice set another record. He scored fifty goals in fifty games even though he had played half the season with an injured knee.

Maurice was just as tenacious off the ice as he was on it. One day in December 1944, Lucille and Maurice had arranged to move to a new apartment. Georges Norchet and some friends were going to help with the move, but they were late arriving.

"I hope they get here soon, Lucille," said Maurice anxiously. "I have to play tonight and I'm determined to have us settled in our new home before then."

When the friends finally did arrive, Maurice knew that they would finish before the game only if he worked extra hard. Even though he would need all his strength and energy that night, he spent the afternoon carrying boxes and furniture up and down stairs.

By the time he got to the Forum for the game, Maurice was almost too tired to lace up his skates.

Maurice's teammates noticed something was wrong. So did Coach Irvin. "What's the matter with the Rocket?" he asked.

"I moved house today, Coach. I'm dead tired."

Coach Irvin was furious. "You're supposed to save your energy for important games, not waste it moving."

Maurice was very upset by the coach's words. He decided to prove that nothing could make him too tired to play well.

Maurice skated hard, even though every muscle in his body was aching. By the end of the game, he had scored five goals, leading the Canadiens to victory.

When the team returned to the dressing room, Coach Irvin said: "If you can score that many goals after moving house all afternoon, Maurice, maybe I should get the rest of the team to carry boxes around before the next big game." Everyone laughed, including Maurice.

As the years passed Maurice scored more and more goals. Slapper was proud of Maurice's determination. But Maurice surprised even Slapper on the night of April 8, 1952.

That night the Canadiens were fighting it out with the Boston Bruins. It was the last game of the semi-finals.

As Maurice skated toward the goal with the puck, two Bruins charged at him. He fell, cracking his head against another player's knee and twisting his neck. Maurice slumped to the ice, unconscious. The crowd fell silent. Was the Rocket badly hurt?

Minutes later the team doctors carried Maurice to the Forum's first aid room. The gash in his head had to be stitched up. When he regained consciousness, the doctors pleaded with Maurice to go to the hospital, but he refused. "I have to get back to the game," he told them. "I can't let the team down now."

By the time he returned to the ice, the score was tied, one to one, and there were only four minutes left to play.

Maurice was dizzy as he stepped onto the ice. He could hear the crowd cheer but he didn't know why. Although his vision was blurry, he saw the puck glide by and off he went after it. Within seconds he was in front of the Bruins' goal and—slap—the puck shot into the net.

The crowd's cheers were deafening. The Rocket had done it again. The final score was three for the Canadiens and one for the Bruins. Thanks to Maurice, the Canadiens had won the game *and* the series!

The next morning Maurice's head hurt and he could hardly remember his spectacular tie-breaking goal.

Slapper told him what had happened. When he had finished Maurice said, "I guess you were right about tenacity, Slapper. If you really want to do something you just have to keep at it."

"That's right, Maurice," said Slapper, "but, you know, you really had me worried last night. It's dangerous to keep on playing or working if you are badly hurt or sick."

"Oh, I know that," said the Rocket. "But I could just feel that my injury wasn't really serious."

Early in the next season, Maurice was just two goals short of matching the record of 324 goals set by a hockey player named Nels Stewart.

The Canadiens were playing in Toronto, and Maurice knew that Nels Stewart would be in the stands, watching the game. He wanted very badly to equal Stewart's record that night. Could he do it?

As usual, the Toronto crowd booed when Maurice stepped onto the ice. Not surprisingly, they had little love for their chief rivals' top player.

Eleven minutes after the game started, Maurice grabbed the puck, swooped down the ice and scored.

Slapper was amazed to hear cheers from the crowd. "Come on, Maurice," someone called, "you can do it. Just one more goal."

Six minutes later, Maurice sizzled the puck into the net again.

The Toronto fans forgot team rivalries in their admiration of Maurice's achievement. They cheered, whistled and stamped their feet as two of Maurice's teammates hoisted him onto their shoulders and paraded him slowly around the ice.

That goal made Maurice a hockey superstar. From then on, the Forum crowds cheered wildly whenever he stepped onto the ice. And after every game, fans waited outside the Canadiens' dressing room to get the Rocket's autograph. He was as much of a hero for his fans as Toe Blake had once been for him.

But no matter how famous he became, Maurice never bragged. When a reporter asked him if he was proud of his goal scoring, Maurice shook his head.

"I never play well enough to be pleased with myself," he explained. "If I get three, four goals, I know that one or two of them have been lucky ones. You can't be proud of yourself for luck, can you?"

However modest Maurice was, his teammates and fans knew that the Rocket had a lot more than just luck. What made him special was his determination to play his best for his team, even if he was tired and hurt and winning seemed impossible. They knew Maurice Richard was a fighter. Maurice Richard had incredible tenacity.

Sometimes, though, Maurice's determination to win went too far, and he would get into fights with players on opposing teams. After one of these fights, in March 1955, Clarence Campbell, the president of the hockey league, refused to let Maurice play for the rest of the season. That even included the playoffs!

When Maurice's fans heard the news they were furious. Campbell's decision ruined Maurice's chance of winning, for the first time in his career, the high-scoring championship of the league. Not only that, but it probably also destroyed the Canadiens' chance of winning the Stanley Cup.

At the next game, Maurice watched from the stands as angry fans showered Clarence Campbell with eggs and rotten vegetables. Someone threw a tear gas bomb into the crowd and everyone began coughing and gasping for breath. The game was cancelled. The angry crowd spilled out onto the street, where they broke windows of the Forum and overturned cars.

The next afternoon Maurice went on the radio and television. He told his fans: "Please make no more trouble. I will take my punishment and be back next year to help the team win the Stanley Cup."

The Rocket's fans were still angry about his suspension, but they admired Maurice so much they did as he asked. The rioting ended.

Over the next few years, Maurice broke nearly every hockey record that had ever been set. The most important milestone as far as he was concerned was his 500th goal.

"I want to dedicate my 500th goal to Dick Irvin, the man who taught me everything I know about hockey," he told reporters after the game. Coach Irvin had died a few months earlier.

About this time, Maurice had the pleasure of welcoming his young brother, Henri, to the Canadiens. The Pocket Rocket, as Henri was soon being called, was fifteen years younger than Maurice and small for a professional hockey player.

At first Maurice tried to protect Henri, but he soon realized that Henri was tough enough and a good enough player to make it on his own.

For the next few years the two Richards played on the same line. Maurice took as much pride in his brother's accomplishments as he did in his own.

The time came when Maurice noticed that he couldn't skate as fast or play for as long as he once had. He didn't want to disappoint his fans, so after scoring 544 goals for the Canadiens, Maurice "the Rocket" Richard retired.

Montrealers, Canadians and hockey fans all around the world were sad to see the Rocket retire. His eighteen outstanding years with the Canadiens were acknowledged when he was named "Hockey Athlete of the Decade." Maurice was also made a member of the Order of Canada.

At a sports dinner in New York, Maurice and several other famous athletes were honored for their "high principles and achievement in sports." In Montreal, a new sports arena was named "Maurice Richard Arena."

Perhaps the most important honor of all to Maurice was his nomination to the Hockey Hall of Fame the year after he retired.

At the ceremony naming him to the Hall of Fame, Clarence Campbell, the man who had once suspended Maurice, praised his tenacity.

"We all have a lesson to learn from Maurice Richard; that with complete and utter dedication to our work we can accomplish great things. Never have I met a man with such singleness of purpose and so completely dedicated to his profession."

Clarence Campbell spoke for all those other Canadians who admired the Rocket even more for his tenacity than for his skill as a hockey player.

You won't all be hockey superstars like Rocket Richard when you grow up. But if you do your very best, and keep at it no matter how much you'd like to give up, then one day, like Maurice Richard, you too will discover the rewards of tenacity.

The End

Maurice Richard was one of Canada's first hockey superstars. His skill, his fighting spirit and, most of all, his refusal to give up even when he was injured earned him the respect of Canadians and sports fans the world over.

Born in Montreal, Quebec, on August 4, 1921, Maurice was the oldest of eight children. His father, Onésime, a machinist for the Canadian Pacific Railway, was an ardent sports lover. He encouraged his sons to play hockey; Maurice was given his first pair of skates when he was four.

The east-end neighborhood of Montreal where the Richards lived was hockey crazy. Although most people didn't have enough money to attend the Montreal Canadiens' games at the Forum, they listened to games broadcast on the radio (there was no television at that time) and they went to matches between local teams.

Like most of his friends, young Maurice had a bad case of hockey fever. He spent every spare minute practicing skating or playing hockey with friends. He also played peewee and, later, midget and bantam hockey for his school, Saint-François-de-Laval.

Maurice grew up during the Depression, when jobs were scarce. To make certain he had a chance of finding one when he finished school, he enrolled in a machinist's course at Montreal Technical High School. In his free time, he played hockey for the high school and for several other local teams. Often he would play two games a night after a full day at school.

By the time he was eighteen, Maurice was an excellent hockey player. That season he played with a team called La Paquette. The team scored 144 goals during the season. Maurice scored 133 of them! His talent brought him to the attention of other coaches, and it wasn't long before Maurice was given a chance to play for the Canadien Seniors, one of the amateur teams of the Montreal Canadiens. No one could have been happier than Maurice, but his happiness didn't last long. In his first game with the Seniors he broke his ankle. It was the first of many injuries that would threaten his career.

MAURICE RICHARD
1921-

However, Maurice would not give up. With the encouragement of his wife, Lucille Norchet, whom he married in 1942, he returned after each injury to play even better hockey than he had before.

The Montreal Canadien's coach, Dick Irvin, recognized and admired Maurice's tenacity and invited him to play with the team. Within a few years, Maurice's incredible perseverance had captured the imagination of hockey fans across the country. Nowhere were they more enthusiastic than in his hometown, Montreal.

Maurice's skill and speed on the ice had earned him the nickname of "the Rocket." Sometimes that name seemed better suited to his temper. Once a burst of temper during a game at the Forum led to a fight, after which Maurice was suspended. His loyal fans were furious. They began to riot and stopped only when their hero asked them to.

Maurice Richard never disappointed his fans. Often he surpassed their expectations. No matter how badly hurt or tired he was, he refused to give up. His tenacity often led the Canadiens to victory even when defeat seemed inevitable.

When he retired in 1960, partly to spend more time with his wife and six children, he was a national hero. Of the many awards he received, he was perhaps most honored by his nomination to the Hockey Hall of Fame only one year after he retired.

Maurice Richard no longer plays hockey, but it continues to be one of his great loves. And, although he no longer leads the Canadiens to victory, he remains a hero to those who remember his tenacity and courage on the ice.

The ValueTale Series